PHOTOGRAPHY by N. JANE ISELEY

Charleston Impressions

TEXT by WILLIAM P. BALDWIN

LEGACY PUBLICATIONS

We would like to thank the residents of Charleston as well as the preservation-conscious custodians, staff and directors we encountered for graciously sharing their city with us. A special thanks to Katharine Robinson and Winslow Hastie of the Historic Charleston Foundation for their guidance and encouragement. Also thanks to our friends at Legacy Publications— Bonnie McElveen-Hunter, Leigh Ann Klee, Kimberly Cote, Carrie Pacifico, David Brown and Laura Archer —for producing another excellent book.

Producer | Alice Turner Michalak
Design | Jaimey Easler, CJE3 Graphic Design
Editor | Chad Kirtland
Proofreaders | Ben Anderson, Karen Disner, Sarah Lindsay, Anne-Marie Thompson

ISBN 978-0-933101-27-2
Library of Congress Catalog Card Number 2011936626

Printed in China by Everbest Printing Co., Ltd

*This book is dedicated to Dorothy Barnwell Kerrison and Agnes LeLand Baldwin,
who over the years inspired us with their knowledge and love of Charleston.*

CHARLESTON is a place where people pause, smile and nod. They hold doors open. They wave to strangers. Don't be surprised. Year after year Charleston is voted the most well-mannered city in the nation, and often the friendliest. Truth be told, being polite is just part of the city's old-timey charms.

To properly enjoy these charms, one must slow down. The scent of tea olive, the blush on a rose, a sea breeze that sets the feathery mimosa to swaying—these pleasures require a change of pace. Charleston is a place of cobblestone streets and pealing church bells, mottled stucco walls giving way to decorative iron and forests of camellias. What's the point of entering an 18th-century townscape if you can't leave behind 21st-century urgency? Meals here are leisurely affairs. Sip. Savor. Have a second glass of sweet tea. Don't miss a carriage ride, and the shuttle bus service is excellent, but don't hesitate to walk. Along with its friendly demeanor, Charleston is also constructed on a very human scale.

For a newcomer, crossing the high expanse of the Cooper River Ravenel Bridge often brings surprise. Charleston is not a city. Charleston is a town. A green canopy of trees covers much of the peninsula. There are no skyscrapers. Not even close. A handful of large buildings house the hospitals, hotels and apartments. The remainder are two- and three-story shops and dwellings with red-tin and blue-tile roofs. The whole expanse is interrupted at intervals only by soaring church steeples. The streets are narrow, the alleys even narrower, and straight can go to crooked in the blink of an eye. Again, it is an Old World landscape.

Water surrounds us: the Ashley River to the south, the Cooper to the north. The old joke goes that they meet to form the Atlantic. That's not quite true, but they do create a tremendous harbor, quite literally a harbor of history. In the far distance sits Fort Sumter, where the Yankee half of the Civil War began. On the far bank of the Cooper rests the massive USS *Yorktown*. On the Charleston side, bending cranes betray a still-working port. Beyond, miles of waterfront parks and promenades await.

It's been said, "Charleston in the spring is like a new bride." Charleston is a garden, and a gardening town. Azalea, dogwood and wisteria blossoms spill through black iron fences. There's no off time for palmettos, live oaks or magnolias. Every season has its flowering, leaf-changing rewards. And speaking of gardens, my old friend, gardener Emily Whaley, once said, "I'll tell you what tourism has done for Charleston. In the old days, we had two decent restaurants. Now we have dozens and dozens." We could also add the city's growing list of world-class events: Spoleto's celebration of the arts, the Southeastern Wildlife Expo and more.

The Cooper River Bridge Run now draws 40,000 contestants. Charleston was just voted the nation's best tennis destination. We have a world-class aquarium. The art galleries rival those of Santa Fe. *Condé Nast Traveler* recently named us the No. 2 U.S. travel destination. San Francisco is first, but that can change. *Travel and Leisure* readers just voted Charleston their second favorite U.S. city. New York is first. Look out, NYC. Lawdy, Lawd. I've preached go slow, and already I'm ahead of myself. This is Charleston.

A SHORT HISTORY

Charleston was no accident, not exactly. The mostly English settlers of 1670 were headed for Beaufort, but the friendly Kiawah Indians convinced them that the banks of the Ashley provided safer refuge. Ten years later they crossed over to the present peninsular site. They'd come here to make fortunes and in some instances to escape religious persecution. The colony was a proprietorship, a gift from the king to his friends, one of whom was Lord Anthony Ashley Cooper, hence the river names. Cooper's secretary, John Locke, drew up a land division based on aristocracy, with a distinctly agricultural bent. Instead, the early settlers traded with the Indians, ran cattle in the woods and produced ship stores.

Eventually they did plant. Rice plantations brought the earliest wealth. Being labor-intensive, they also brought vastly more imported slaves. Indigo later did the same. Finally, cotton —especially the fine, long staple grown along the seashore— brought even more wealth and slaves. Carolina was a true agrarian culture. It's sometimes argued that Charleston (then called Charles Towne) was a secondary outcome of this early land

The scent of tea olive, the blush on a rose, a sea breeze that sets the feathery mimosa to swaying—these pleasures require a change of pace. Charleston is a place of cobblestone streets and pealing church bells, mottled stucco walls giving way to decorative iron and forests of camellias.

settlement scheme. On the eve of the American Revolution, the "planters" who lived in Charleston only for the "season" still looked down on the year-round "merchants." But both were prosperous members of the upper class. They were this country's statesmen. They sent their sons off to England to be educated and hoped to marry their daughters to European nobility. Fine coaches and thoroughbred horses were imported. Fine furniture was sent from overseas, but there was little need; Charleston had some of the world's finest cabinet makers. Wig makers, dressmakers, silversmiths, portrait painters and master builders were all well employed. Charleston was the country's richest city, and its most cultured. The gentry enjoyed horse races, grand balls, banquets, music recitals, operas and, of course, the theater. One of our nation's first libraries was founded here in 1748. Twelve years earlier, the country's first theater presented *The Recruiting Officer*, a ribald and well-received farce. The first truly functioning railroad came along in the next century, followed by the first shot of the Civil War. But again I've jumped ahead.

Amid this extravagance, death was an everyday occurrence. The odds against early settlers were frightening. Malarial fevers took their toll on the youngest and oldest and drained the energy of all. The poorer whites resented their richer betters. Both lived in fear of the enslaved African servants, who lived in fear of them. The city was both a fortress and a graveyard. Happily, that's changed. The city of now is not the city of then. Still, we walk streets that have changed little in the last 100 and sometimes 200 years. The buildings crowding in on all sides are not fanciful reconstructions but the real thing. We saunter where pirates sauntered. The Swamp Fox, General Francis Marion, leaped from one Charleston balcony; General George Washington spoke from another. Duels were fought on these greens. Cannonballs clipped tree branches and tombstones. Courtships were pressed, marriages made, babies born. Lucky people grew old. Life was lived here.

Someone once told me, "Just remember Charleston was a defense project, not a housing project." The proprietors laid out Charleston according to a Grand Model, a fortified stronghold enclosing a few fairly wide, straight streets, a square, a few public buildings and a church. A protective wall was built by the early 1700s. Cannons, a moat and a drawbridge added more defenses. Occasionally the French and Spanish would mount an invasion, none remotely successful. The pirates were more resourceful. But eventually a few dozen were hung along the seawall as a deterrent, their bodies left to rot. The Indians proved the most successful attackers. In 1714 the Yemassee drove to within 10 miles of the city gates, killing all they came across.

Still, the greatest threat loomed within the city walls. The fear of slave revolt kept Charleston a garrisoned city long after she'd grown beyond her walls. As to vestiges, the most prominent is the High Battery. Famed today as a place to walk and catch the sea breeze, this was a military battery. Look to the cannons on the landward side. From there and from the new parks, you can see Fort Sumter, Fort Johnson, Castle Pinckney and Fort Moultrie. The old Citadel Building on Marion Square was built on the city's outskirts in response to a planned slave rebellion. A section of the late wall remains, as does a fragment of an early bastion in the basement of the Exchange Building. The Powder Magazine dates from 1704. The world's first functioning submarine, the *Hunley*, has recently been raised from the harbor entrance and will soon be on display.

CITY PLANNING

Our streets can admittedly be confusing. I was born here, and 66 years later I'll still find myself about to enter a one-way street the wrong way. Charleston writer John Bennett said, "The names of Charleston streets are often changed and hardly ever to the better." Ripley's Believe It or Not labeled King Street the nation's longest street of retail sales. It started out as The Broad Path, an Indian right of way that led to the Mississippi River. Lined today with lawyers' offices and art galleries, Broad Street was a broad 63 feet wide and was one of the few to keep its name. Church Street was New Church until the Presbyterians built a meeting house and changed the first Church Street to Meeting Street. Chalmers was the street Bennett had in mind. As Union Alley, it was famed for prostitution and rum drinking. It was changed to Chalmers to correct that. Apparently, it's worked. I suspect the Union of Union Alley comes not from the Union that Abraham Lincoln forced on us nor the unity related to church services. I'd guess it celebrates the 1707 union of Scotland and England. Tradd Street is an early lane named possibly for the colony's first native-born child. Nearby Water Street was once a creek that marked the lower boundary of the town. Market Street was the opposite boundary. It too was a creek, but was filled and became the meat market. Calhoun was once Boundary Street, for this was the town limits; likewise Line Street, a century later. East Bay faced the bay. The area between the street and harbor, now built up as a beautiful waterfront park, was once wharfs. I can recall ship chandleries still doing business on East Bay.

A city grows, shrinks, shifts and shapes. It's an organic experience, or should be. Man proposes. God disposes. Hurricanes have washed across this peninsula at least a dozen times. The Lowcountry is low. Make no mistake. Avoid the Cross Town when heavy rains coincide with high tide. The Great Fire of 1861 caused massive destruction. A major earthquake struck in 1886, toppling church towers and sheering off the fronts of buildings. The familiar "earthquake bolts" date from this time, as do the stuccoed walls, for it was simpler to plaster over cracked brick than to replace it. Toward the end of the Civil War the lower portions of the city were so badly battered they were abandoned altogether. Charleston was always partly burning to the ground and rebuilding itself. A sharp architectural eye can trace the paths of these blazes across the peninsula.

The early call for a well-ordered city with wide straight streets quickly went astray. Lot owners wanting to maximize their profits or just make room for descendants created narrow alleys. Meeting Street couldn't continue straight out of town because pirate hunter Colonel William Rhett built his house in the way. Narrow King Street served instead. As mansions replaced simpler dwellings, neighborhoods of distinction grew, then became unfashionable and decayed. The black slave population lived cheek to jowl with their white owners in the

> *We walk down streets that have changed little in the last 100 and sometimes 200 years. The buildings crowding in on all sides are not fanciful reproductions but the real thing. We saunter where pirates sauntered. Duels were fought on these greens. Cannonballs clipped tree branches and tombstones.*

yard's slave quarters. Cattle, goats and chickens were added to the mix. I was surprised when a below-Broad resident in her 80s told me that the first sound of the morning was not the familiar call of the shrimp vendor: "I got shrimps, I got shrimps." Rather, it was the crowing of the gamecocks a block down.

In 1980 my mother bought a townhouse on Adgers Wharf. A wharf no longer. The lane is of cobblestones and the "row houses" are carved from a converted pre-Revolution warehouse, with brick walls 28 inches thick and exposed beams 4 inches by 16 inches. Charleston rightly claims to have invented historic preservation in this country. Along with that goes a particularly aggressive adaptive approach to architecture. Today people live in former shops, kitchens and carriage houses. A rice mill can be an office building and a railway loading station a supermarket. The Old Citadel is a hotel, and there are plans to make the Rivers Federal Building one as well.

ARCHITECTURE

Charleston's earliest architecture was distinctly English and distinctly urban. There are no references to log cabins. More likely, early builders used post-and-beam construction with sticks and clay between the gaps. With cypress and pine plentiful, wood construction was a favorite. But the threat of runaway fires brought repeated demands for brick houses. Good clay, and hence good brick, was readily available. Still, a wood house was not only cheaper but more comfortable to live in. Beyond the city walls, wood frame was favored. Foundations were of brick, stone ballast or oyster shell tabby. Chimneys were of brick. Floors were heart pine. Window sashes are referred to in the early 1700s. Interior woodwork done by master carvers was common until the 19th century when plastering came into fashion. Roofs were of cypress shakes, then tile, and finally raised soldered tin came into fashion. Occasionally repair work reveals layers of all three.

House design adapted traditional European needs and taste to a tropical climate. One-, two- and three-story rectangles and hip-roofed square buildings entered directly from the street were the rule at the beginning of the Georgian period, that time of King George before the Revolution. As is common to much domestic architecture, these could be a single room wide or two: hence single houses and double houses. The single house became uniquely Charlestonian. Turned narrowways to the street, these dwellings featured a long piazza or porch to shade the sun and create private outdoor living spaces. A drive led from the street down the side to a rear yard where carriage houses, slave quarters and livestock could be found. The interior was divided by a central hallway and stair running to the second and often third story. Faced to catch

Decorative iron can imbue simple structures with elegance. Adorn a plain home with a basic balcony, and the marriage creates a thing of beauty. Fanciful Victorian intricacies add new depth to a staid Federalist facade. The scrolls of a wrought iron gate add romantic mystery to a guarded garden.

the sea breeze, these houses were cool. Architectural historian Sam Stoney claimed they were "trimmed like a sail whenever it was possible to square against the course of this most favorable breezes." Not sharing a common wall with their neighbor, they were safer from fire. And more private. To be separate from your neighbor suited the Charlestonian's independent spirit. Indeed, there were numerous variations on this single house layout, and by the mid-19th century the form had even been applied to mansions.

Houses grow over the centuries, additions are made, renovations in the newest style (a process sometimes reversed these days). Be on your guard when reading local house styles. Charleston has hundreds of examples of the small sturdy Georgian dwellings— Tradd Street comes to mind. The double house was more aptly suited to the celebration of wealth, however, and she has more than her share of these solid but elegant Georgian structures as well—the Miles Brewton House the most outstanding. In the Federalist period that followed, homes slimmed and grew more ornate. England's Adams brothers influenced building.

Charleston's gifted amateur Gabriel Manigault became the leading architect, designing for his brother Joseph Manigault and City Hall. The 19th century brought even more architectural exuberance. America's first native-born architect, Robert Mills, a fan of Greek Revival and Neoclassical styles, is best known locally for the heavy columned First Baptist Church (and nationally for the Washington Monument). These "temples" became a favorite for churches and banks. Next came the more exotic revivals, especially the Italianate with its brackets and arches, and the Gothic with even more arches and soaring crenulated toppings. E.B. White and the partnership of Francis D. Lee and Edward C. Jones were the best known of these architects. The Victorian architecture that followed required less symmetry but an equal amount of invention. Though poor by the nation's standards, Charleston still managed to have her share of great mansard-roofed mansions and delicate Queen Anne bungalows. Beyond that, Charleston is happily lacking. There was no money for the urban revitalization experienced elsewhere in the country. Charleston enjoyed a moratorium on 20th-century progress, and preservation groups saw that this continued—a subject to which we'll return.

IRONWORK

Charleston's flourishing ironwork is an indelible part of the city's image. Decorative iron can inbue simple structures with elegance. Adorn a plain home with a basic balcony, and the marriage creates a thing of beauty. Fanciful Victorian intricacies give new depth to a staid Federalist façade. The scrolls of a wrought-iron gate add romantic mystery to a guarded garden.

The placement of Charleston's early residences and its tropical climate necessitated the ironwork that followed. Builders set Charleston's homes back on their lots. The resulting side yards required substantial gates and fences for security. Settlers quickly learned that the damp conditions wreaked havoc on wooden balconies, railing and fences. The prevalence of fire also made forged metal a practical alternative.

Decorative ironwork can be found in many early American cities, but not all ironwork is equal. Authentic wrought iron is heated and worked by hand with a hammer. Popularized in Europe in the 1600s, this method likely made its way to Charleston through pieces that arrived with French and English settlers. Charleston's earliest examples of wrought iron date to the Revolutionary War. The process was probably in use earlier, but older examples have been lost. Some were likely requisitioned during war times. By contrast, cast iron is melted and poured into molds of nearly any shape. During Victorian times, this became a popular substitute for the more traditional hammered style. Work from this time often showcases the theatrical whimsy of the age. Some ironwork traditionalists refer to cast iron as the plastic of its time. From the 1840s on, balconies, columns, lampposts, gates and more were made by this modern method. By that time, however, Charleston's many impressive wrought-iron gates and balconies were in place, and locals came to prefer the earlier process.

Too often, we don't know the craftsmen behind these great works. Three German blacksmiths, J.A.W. Iusti, Frederic Ortmann and Christopher Werner, were widely known for their work in the 1800s. Ortmann's sons continued to work into the 20th century. Jacob Roh also left a legacy of work throughout the city. African-American men worked in these shops from the earliest days. One of these, Philip Simmons, emerged as Charleston's foremost ironworker of the 20th century.

Charleston's grand ironworks abound; think church gates and balconies. But the intensity and intricacy of this craft also shine through in the careful lines of a simple handrail or the play of light upon a tapering spiral's tip. Look around and you'll find that Charleston's ironwork surrounds you—lamps, boot scrapers, grilles, signs—all of it contributing to the city's architectural signature.

PRESERVATION

Many believe that Charleston's fight to save its architectural heritage can be traced largely to one woman, Susan Pringle Frost, suffragette, social conscience and preservationist par excellence. To keep buildings from being razed for business sites and to stop the dismantling of historic interiors by outsiders, she purchased buildings in a piecemeal fashion. Her selfless, if somewhat haphazard, real estate dealings would make her the "Angel of Tradd Street" and the protector of Church Street, St. Michael's Alley and the Miles Brewton House. The Preservation Society of Charleston, which she helped form, saved the Joseph Manigault house and many others. The oldest community-based preservation society in America, this group now oversees zoning ordinances, conducts house and garden tours, works with schools and neighborhood groups to extend the preservation concept in new directions, and more. In the 1940s Frances Edmunds began a related effort that systematized and broadened the base of preservation efforts. Her Historic Charleston Foundation was established with a revolving fund that could be used to purchase and restore buildings that would then be resold. The resurrection of the entire Ansonborough neighborhood was its most successful project, and the foundation is now concentrating on renewing other neighborhoods in a manner that allows the poorer residents to remain. The foundation also runs two museum houses, the Charleston International Antiques Show, and the Festival of Houses and Gardens tours. The Charleston Museum and the city also have a long history of preservation work. All organizations act in conjunction with the city's Board of Architectural Review and various other agencies to create a protective shield over the historic district.

Historians sometimes cast doubt on the sincerity of early Charlestonians' faith and suggest the churches were simply extensions of social and financial hierarchies. One Quaker questioned how earnest a prayer could be made when it was preceded by the statement, "Here, hold my cards while I go to prayer."

THE HOLY CITY

In terms of architecture, Charleston lives up to her title "The Holy City." Setting off for the backcountry, Methodist circuit rider Bishop Francis Asbury mocked Charlestonians who raced to build the highest steeple. Early Anglican (later Episcopal) churches were influenced by Christopher Wren's distinctively steepled English churches. The Greek Revival movement (the Greek temple)

dominated 18th-century Charleston—especially the Baptist and Methodist congregations. The Gothic style came in the mid-1800s; there are several examples, notably the French Huguenot Church and Grace Episcopal on Wentworth Street.

Historians sometimes cast doubts on the sincerity of early Charlestonians' faith and suggest the churches were simply extensions of social and financial hierarchies. Writing around 1750, one Quaker questioned how earnest a prayer could be made when it was preceded by the statement, "Here, hold my cards while I go to prayer." Still, in the early centuries, the colony's founders hoped to avoid the bloody religious controversy that had racked Europe. With the exception of Catholicism, all faiths were welcomed. William Sayle, the first governor of Carolina, saw the wilderness before him as a place to settle "millions" of Presbyterians. After the revocation of Huguenots' rights in 1685, shiploads of French Protestants exchanged their neat villages and farms for the Lowcountry swamplands. William Screven brought a party of Baptists down from Maine. Returning from a failed Scotch settlement in Central America, Rev. Archibald Stobo was literally "shipwrecked" in Charleston and founded Presbyterian churches. The Anglicans, the established Church of England, dominated politically and economically. In 1706 French Huguenots and Barbadian settlers united to pass the Church Act, which established the Anglican Church of England as the official state church. Midway through the century an influx of Germans brought their Lutheran devotion. Jewish settlers arrived early and enjoyed a freedom of worship denied them in the Old World. One Charleston synagogue began what is now the Reform Jewish movement. Only the Catholic Church was discouraged, for England still reeled from its break with that tradition. More importantly, the much-reviled Spanish were indivisibly Catholic. Around 1790, the Catholic aversion subsided somewhat, and the increasing Irish population joined with refugees from the French Islands to found a community of faith. Last to have a formal standing were the African-American churches, for these required the fighting of a war and the freeing of the slaves to finally become established. As to sincerity, then and now, each and every church, meeting house and temple strikes me as a sacred place, and Charleston seems as holy a city as any other.

> *Charleston was a garden waiting to happen. The Gulf Stream bends close here, and the same warmth that helped cultivate sea island cotton facilitated a long growing season and demanded outdoor "tropical" living. The Florida Maritime forest of this area is thick with live oaks, magnolia, dogwood and palmetto.*

GARDENS

"A garden is meant to keep the tigers out," Emily Whaley used to tell me. Much earlier, in 1682, Thomas Ashe wrote, "Their gardens also began to be beautiful and adorned with such Herbs and Flowers which to the Smell or Eye are pleasing and agreeable, viz; the Rose, Tulip, Carnation and Lilly, Etc." No doubt a homesickness for England led to the cultivation of these favorites.

Carolina was founded by botanizers, men and women who were fascinated with what they found growing here and quickly sent examples back. As late as 1754, Dr. Alexander Garden, who gave his name to the gardenia, was still making discoveries. Sea captains and diplomats carried plant wealth in both directions. Joel Poinsett brought the poinsettia back with him from Mexico. The French explorer Michaux gave us the camellia. Merchant Henry Laurens kept a large garden.

Even before them, Charleston was a garden waiting to happen. The Gulf Stream bends close here, and the same warmth that helped cultivate sea island cotton facilitated a long growing season and demanded outdoor "tropical" living. The Florida Maritime forest of this area is thick with live oaks, magnolia, dogwood, sweet bay, palmetto, wax myrtle, jessamine and cassina. Add to that the Spanish moss, natural ferns and ivies and you have a ready-made garden, or at least a fine underpinning. To this colonists quickly added tea olive, wisteria, camellias, azaleas, roses, jasmine, oleander, hydrangeas, banana shrub and hundreds more.

Early Charleston mansions had formal European gardens laid out in geometrical perfection. Using early plot plans, many of these have been restored—the Nathaniel Russell and Joseph Manigault houses come to mind. In modern times these narrow spaces have blossomed into some of the city's best-loved gardens. There's a particular craft involved here—finding the sun for roses, borrowing the landscape from your neighbor's live oak and creating a private escape on a quarter acre of land or less. The Historic Charleston Foundation is particularly adept at showing these off during their annual spring tours.

Of course, the larger plantation gardens surrounding the city deserve equal mention. By the end of the 19th century, steamboat excursions carried Yankee visitors up the Ashley River to visit the extensive gardens of Magnolia Plantation and Middleton Place. The first was laid out in the late Romantic manner, which took best advantage of the existing landscape; the second followed the earlier formal tradition. Little has changed at either. Both remain open to the public, and for garden enthusiasts they are must sees. On the opposite side of the city, Boone Hall also boasts a wonderful garden. Professional landscape gardeners are occasionally employed. The best known of the last hundred years were Loutrel Briggs, who crafted several hundred gardens or "spots" in the area, and Robert Marvin, best known for his work on the neighboring Sea Islands.

CEMETERIES

Early churchyards served as burial grounds. The closer you could be buried to the church wall, the better your chances of getting into heaven. To be buried beneath the church floor ensured the best chance of all. We still find these church graveyards scattered throughout the city, often filled with ancient, moss-trimmed stones piled together in profusion. The earliest markers were carved from cypress planks. By 1700 carved stones were being imported from Boston, and Charleston may have the most extensive example of this art form outside Boston. Portraits provided a favorite motif on the stones. Skulls and bones and related reminders of mortality adorned others. The oldest gates into St. Philip's (now gone) were crowned with a warning of this nature. As tastes changed, urns and wreaths came into fashion as well as chestlike vaults such as the one sheltering the grave of John C. Calhoun. Tombstone inscriptions, often the last chance to set the record straight, make for entertaining reading.

By the 1820s science suggested that crowding a city with the bodies of previous inhabitants lead to fevers and hence more burials. Planners then constructed municipal cemeteries on the outskirts of town, often laid out as parklike gardens. Magnolia Cemetery is an excellent example (beside it are Catholic, Jewish and Lutheran versions). Reflecting ponds surrounded by Oriental bridges, moss-draped oaks and azaleas complement an impressive collection of 19th- and 20th-century tombstone art.

THE PEOPLE

"Charleston is owned by the Germans and run by the Irish," quipped a late 19th-century visitor. Today, the city is still run by the Irish; some would say run well. German Lutherans and Irish Catholics made up a large block of the citizenry. Charleston had its own German language newspapers. German bankers and investors owned much of the city. On the other hand, the mayors of Charleston were often Irish.

Reading early commentaries, we might envision a city occupied only by an English aristocracy allied with French Huguenot merchants, both being waited on by African servants. In fact, antebellum Charleston also housed Jews, Italians, Irish, Scots, French Catholics and Germans. Notably, Charleston also became a place for Yankees. Business was beneath the dignity of the planter aristocracy; by the 1820s most leading merchants were northerners. However, Charleston was and still is English in its orientation. Charleston saw herself as a Little London and followed London fashions closely. As then, the essential values of liberty, family and land endure.

Each new set of arrivals left their mark. This is particularly true of the Africans. The word "Gullah" once applied to a particular tribe or area in Africa, and the slaves so designated were valued for their knowledge of rice cultivation. Gradually the name was applied to the entire black culture, one marked by a distinct language, crafts and cuisine. Gullah cooking is still celebrated in many restaurants, making excellent use of rice and locally caught seafood. "Gullah cooking is about family and rice," said Frank Jenkins, owner of one of the area's excellent Gullah restaurants. Taking one of the many "Gullah" tours is a must.

It's hard to pigeonhole charm, to rate and scale it, to put it between covers. It's difficult to catalogue quiet or even noisy joys. Hard facts might be a hindrance. A historian sees one thing, an artist another, a traveler a third and so on. The Charleston you'll experience is already inside of you. Trust me, it is. And that's how it should be. Just be sure to let that inside be fully exposed. The world is full of cities, but there's only one Charleston. Enjoy.

A historian sees one thing, an artist another, a traveler a third and so on. The Charleston you'll experience is already inside of you. Trust me, it is. And that's how it should be. Just be sure to let that inside be fully exposed. The world is full of cities, but there is only one Charleston. Enjoy.

The Pineapple Fountain (*previous spread*)
Imported from the Caribbean, pineapples were a great luxury and hence became
a symbol of warmth and welcome. They often crowned gateposts. This modern
version bubbles out a greeting.

The South Carolina Aquarium
A favorite family destination, the aquarium offers solid environmental lessons
disguised as fun. Hypnotic.

The Vendue Fountain
This splashy spot along the waterfront provides a favorite summertime escape
for Charleston children seeking relief from the seasonal heat.

The Custom House
Completed in 1879, the Custom House features a granite basement and two upper floors of marble. The original plan was far more ambitious, but the Civil War interrupted construction and the building was scaled down. Still, a strong Federal presence presides, especially when compared to the municipal and state offices. Charleston has many buildings covered in stucco, but few of actual stone.

Maps of Charleston
Want to get your historical bearings? Here's the spot, overlooking the harbor with Fort Sumter in the distance. Charleston has a long tradition of waterfront pleasure grounds. In the 1740s these wharf areas were a favorite promenade—which scandalized proper Londoners. No controversy these days.

Earthquake Bolts (*following spread*)
The Charleston Earthquake of 1886 left much of Charleston once again in ruins. Where brick walls didn't crumble, they cracked. The solution was to apply a coat of stucco and run these earthquake bolts completely through the structures.

Farmers' and Exchange Bank
The antebellum years were culturally conservative, but in 1853 Francis D. Lee designed this brownstone jewelry box, now a restaurant, in the Moorish Revival style.

The Old Exchange and Provost Dungeon
Now open to the public, this dungeon once held pirates and patriot Isaac Hayne. In the lower left is a portion of the original Half-Moon Battery seawall that dates from 1701.

Rainbow Row
Most assume this rainbow of colors dates from early years, but a 20th-century restorer picked these shades. Early Charleston builders used ox blood and indigo to achieve bright hues.

Captain James Missroon House
A portion of the Granville Bastion rests beneath the former home of Captain Missroon, who occupied it until after the Civil War. It now houses the Historic Charleston Foundation.

Edmondston Alston House

This must-see historical attraction is among Charleston's finest museum houses. Located on the High Battery, the home affords excellent views of Charleston Harbor. Built for the Edmondston family in 1825, the mansion received a makeover from the Alstons in 1838. Some years later General P.G.T. Beauregard watched the bombardment of Fort Sumter from the home's piazza.

Edmondston Alston House Library

The house is furnished with Alston family pieces, including furniture, paintings and the beautifully bound volumes that fill this library. They've been in residence since the house was first acquired. This Victorian era desk, the Wooten Secretary, promised "Order reigns supreme, confusion avoided, vexation spared." To the dismay of English cabinetmakers, even Queen Victoria used one of the American-made Wootens.

The Battery
The Battery is a favorite spot for early risers of all persuasions, including dog walkers and photographers. The popular promenade stretches along the Charleston Peninsula where the Cooper and Ashley rivers meet. During the Civil War, the Battery held artillery. Today, joggers and walkers enjoy views of grandiose mansions to one side and Charleston Harbor to the other.

General William Moultrie
Following the Civil War, New England historians downplayed the South's contribution to the Revolutionary War. Southerners added to the neglect by doting on their more recent but failed bid for independence. In 1776 General Moultrie and his troops soundly defeated the British fleet at nearby Sullivan's Island, one of our nation's first substantial victories.

George Eveleigh House
Built below the odd bend in Church Street, this was once waterfront property. However, the slanted shafts weren't, as legend has it, there to tie up boats. The sidewalk was paved with fragile Bermuda stone, and these posts were meant to keep the carriage wheels at bay.

Mrs. Whaley's Garden
Perhaps the best publicized private garden in Charleston. I spent many happy hours sitting here as Emily explained gardening, entertaining and the ways of the Lowcountry world. Those lessons later became a book that we collaborated on, *Mrs. Whaley and Her Charleston Garden.*

Garden Pool

Charleston's courtyards hold many surprises, such as this hidden pool.
Note the First Scots Presbyterian Church bell towers in the far distance.
Famed watercolor artist Alice Huger Smith made this her home.
Perhaps her touch is at work in the pool's reflection.

Church Street Garden

Clipped boxwoods line a formal design popular in Charleston 250 years ago.
Geometrically designed gardens such as this one carried on the traditional European
style. Examples can still be found behind many of Charleston's high fences.

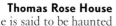

Thomas Rose House
This 1733 stucco-covered brick home is said to be haunted by Dr. Joseph Ladd, who died here after being wounded in a duel fought for an actress named Perdita.

First Baptist Church
It's easy to forget that these 19th-century revival styles were once "modern" architecture. This one was designed by Robert Mills, who also designed the Washington Monument.

Heyward-Washington House
Thomas Heyward signed the Declaration of Independence, and George Washington stayed here in 1791. Among the first homes saved from demolition, it is now open for daily tours.

Pirate House Detail
The pirates had all been hanged by the time this was built in 1740. Beneath the stucco is much-prized Bermuda stone, which was brought here as ship ballast.

Dock Street Theater (*previous spread*)
This amazing renovation was made possible with Depression-era funding.
The original Dock Street Theater was on Queen Street. This building had previously
been the Planter's Hotel, which gave us Planter's Punch. Well-known restorers
Simons and Lapham were the 20th-century architects.

St. Philip's Church
Dating from the 1830s, this Charleston landmark is a quirky combination
of luck and design. Following the fiery destruction of the first church, the
building committee rushed the start here and managed to block half the road.
Architect Edward Brickell White set aside his Modernist leanings and designed
the steeple in a conservative Wren Church style. The brown paint went
on when the brownstone craze reached Charleston.

Catfish Row, Charleston Improvement Corp. Houses
These small Victorian houses were a late addition to the cityscape.
Note not just the frills, but also the gesture toward front yards and porches
that allowed homeowners to chat with passersby. Beyond is Catfish Row,
home of the operatic lovers Porgy and Bess.

Pink House

Among the city's earliest structures, this once held a tavern with a cramped brothel on the upper two floors. I set a novel in the Pink House, but not during that disreputable period.

Chalmers Street Cobblestones

Charleston's streets were notoriously bad. Oyster shells paved some, but thick sand was the norm. Brought as ship ballast, these cobblestones were a tooth-jarring improvement.

Old Slave Mart Museum

In 1856 a city ordinance prohibited the sale of slaves beside the Exchange Building, and a series of these "marts" opened nearby. Auction masters Ryan and Oakes used this one. In 1938 Miriam Wilson purchased the building. This museum of African and African-American arts, crafts and history is operated by her foundation.

Camellias and Washington Square Gate

Hard to believe, but this overthrow (the section above the gate) was considered by one ironwork critic to be too heavily fashioned. When the adjoining bank became the city hall, houses were torn down to form this city park. Camellias were well established by then.

The Powder Magazine

Touted as Charleston's oldest public building, this powder museum hints at the fortifications that once surrounded the city. It was completed in 1713 and used during the Revolutionary War. Now a National Historic Landmark, it operates as a museum.

Calhoun Mansion

With 24,000 square feet and 25 rooms, it's the city's largest private home. Built in 1876, it boasts multicolored brick and Corinthian columns. It can be visited by appointment.

Nathaniel Russell House

The King of the Yankee Merchants built this home in 1808. His initials are scrolled in iron above the door. The Historic Charleston Foundation now operates the house as a museum.

Nathaniel Russell House
Graceful architectural lines are found throughout. This elliptical, free-flying staircase leads to the primary reception rooms on the second floor and beyond.

Nathaniel Russell House Office
This desk hints at the business side of things. Buying and selling were unworthy occupations for Southern aristocrats. New England merchants, like Russell, tended their businesses.

Meeting Street Beagle
This plain 1770s tenement received a high Victorian facelift from one-time owner and contractor Bertram Kramer. The guarding beagle gives a sense of human—or canine—scale.

Brandford-Horry House
William Brandford acquired this land through marriage and built this house prior to the Revolution. His grandson, Elias Horry, added the piazza extending over the sidewalk.

St. Michael's Episcopal Church
Not just a Charleston landmark, but *the* Charleston landmark.
Over the years St. Michael's steeple has served as a lighthouse,
lookout and meteorological observation tower.

South Carolina Society Hall
Gabriel Manigault designed this 1804 building, which housed
a French Huguenot immigrant relief society. The lanterns,
taken from an earlier site, may be the city's oldest ironwork.

The Fireproof Building

This fire-resistant structure was designed by architect Robert Mills to house public records. As the home of the South Carolina Historical Society, it still does. The Peppermint Peach needs no introduction. Note the elaborate ironwork overthrow. Looks perfect.

Hibernian Hall

"Harp of the isle of manly hearts, the land of generous feelings, Thy sacred melody imparts a thousand fond revealing." Early immigrant groups formed societies to aid fellow countrymen as they arrived in the colony. This one may have started as The Sons of Erin. The St. Cecilia Ball is held here, and the St. Patrick's Day Parade makes a visit. The ironwork harp was crafted by Christopher Werner.

A. D. 1840

HIBERNIAN HA

Gibbes Museum of Art
Benevolent James Shoolbred Gibbes endowed this art museum in the late 19th century. The Beaux Arts gallery opened in 1905. Well known for traveling exhibits as well as Charleston originals, The Gibbes has become a favorite tourist destination.

Antique Fire Engines
The Earthquake of 1886 not only started fires; it also destroyed firehouses. Soon after this central station opened, offering ready access in two directions, it housed four steam engine companies. Antique fire engines are now displayed, one dating to those early times.

Circular Congregational Church (*following spread*)
Early Congregationalists and Presbyterians had humble meeting houses, not churches. Hence Church Street became Meeting Street. Robert Mills designed the original circular church that stood on this site. When it burned, this one was built using bricks.

Dragon Gate

The late Robert Jordan's ranking as the "American Tolkien" is suggested by these dragon gates beside his home. His *Wheels of Time* fantasy series was a continual best seller.

Sword Gate

Working in both cast and wrought iron, craftsman Christopher Werner used this design first on the municipal guard building. This was an ancient Roman tradition and another reminder of Charleston's combative reputation.

Robert Pringle House
This home, built for Judge Robert Pringle in 1774, showcases a panopoly of Charleston
architectural styles. It's a Georgian house with a Regency
piazza and Victorian front bay window.

Brick Homes
Window boxes, the ubiquitous crepe myrtle, a pine nut gate topping, wrought-iron gates and lanterns, plus earthquake bolts—a typical Charleston streetscape.

Captain John Morrison House
Sea captain John Morrison retired to Charleston and built an unusually wide single house. The piazzas and elegant entry are of the traditional scale.

Miles Brewton House
Many consider this Georgian mansion, completed in 1769, to be South Carolina's finest house. When the English entered the town during the Revolution, Cornwallis stayed here. Following the Civil War, a Union commander commandeered the same. The gate overthrow is one of the two oldest in the city. The iron spikes above the fence probably date from the threatened Denmark Vesey slave uprising of 1822.

Patrick O'Donnell House
Construction of "O'Donnell's Folly" took so long that the young lady O'Donnell was trying to impress left him for another. Still, the Irish builder's work is a beauty.

Gated Garden
Charleston's gardens offer passers-by a teasing glimpse, in the tradition of the old
Zen master who viewed the mountain through a hole in the fence. Anti-secessionist
Rev. Paul Trapier Gervais lived here, as did novelist Josephine Pinckney.

Cleland Kinloch Huger House Doorway
A Charleston favorite, lyres for the gate. The home of Burnet Rhett Maybank,
former mayor, governor and U.S. senator. The 1857 house was built by Patrick
O'Donnell, the unlucky-in-love Irish contractor.

Pineapple Gate House (*following spread*)
It's called The Pineapple Gate House, and pineapples are the traditional sign
of welcome. However, I believe these are European pine nuts, which luckily have
the same welcoming connotations.

Charleston City Hall

Though there's some debate, this 1801 bank building is credited to amateur
architect Gabriel Manigault—amateur in the sense that he had no formal training.
There's a small Angel Gabriel emblem here for evidence.
It's been serving as City Hall since 1818.

Broad Street toward St. Michael's

A grand variety of Italianate storefronts with St. Michael's Church in the distance.
Built in 1750, this Episcopal Church resembles London's St. Martin-in-the-Field
and remains the city's oldest religious structure.

Four Corners at Dawn
Robert Ripley of Ripley's Believe It or Not designated the corners of Broad and Meeting streets The Four Corners of the Law: the church, the federal post office, the county courthouse and the city hall.

Sleepy Morning on Lenwood Boulevard
A latecomer in a city of ancient streets, Lenwood Boulevard was created in the 20th century. A colorful flowerbox and warm porch set the scene for a lazy day.

John Rutledge House & Col. Thomas Pinckney House

John Rutledge was Charleston's heavy-handed director during the Revolution and earned the nickname "Dictator." Later, the Gadsden family added the wrought-iron front. Last but not least, William Deas, a Rhett family butler, invented she-crab soup here at the beginning of the 20th century. The Col. Thomas Pinckney House, to the right, showcases one of the finest examples of Classical Revival style in the city. Completed in 1829, the mansion was the scene of grand entertainments during the winter social season and features real stone for the portico columns.

John Lining House

One of the city's oldest dwellings, the Lining house often doubled as a pharmacy. Following the Civil War, this was the site of the famed mermaid riots. When persistent rains flooded the countryside, superstitious residents accused the pharmacist of holding a mermaid captive in a jar. Riots ensued. Something was released into the ocean, and the rains stopped.

Unitarian Churchyard (*previous spread*)
Caroline Gilman, antebellum novelist, editor of a children's newspaper and wife of
the minister, laid out this garden among the stones and is credited with planting
some of the crepe myrtles. She's buried in the churchyard.

Fountain at Charleston Place
Back when thoroughbred horses were considered necessities not luxuries,
Charleston was famed for her bloodlines and race tracks.
This fountain is a welcome reminder of those horsey times.

Restaurants At Night
From its earliest days, Charleston was known for its hospitality
and cuisine, but that was most often on a private level.
Today fine restaurants line Meeting Street.

William Aiken House and Garden
A popular wedding spot, the William Aiken House features ample and beautifully landscaped outdoor space for partygoers. The home's namesake founded the South Carolina Canal and Railroad Company.

Bluesteins
If you tire of Bluesteins, you're tired of architecture and life as well. There's all this Italianate business going on. Plus, it's blue.

Central Baptist Church
Built in 1891, Central Baptist Church was the first in the city designed by a black architect. It's also famed for its interior murals and, of course, the bold promise on the steeple.

Aiken-Rhett House
Governor William Aiken remodeled this 1817 mansion in the Italianate manner. Jefferson Davis visited. General Beauregard made his headquarters here. This entry was a late addition.

Aiken-Rhett House
Governor Aiken and his wife traveled through Europe gathering treasures for their
Charleston mansion. The reclining figure is likely the blind beggar girl
of Pompeii, a favorite subject in both Victorian art and literature.

Synagogue of Kahal Kadosh Beth Elohim

When the original synagogue burned in 1838, the congregation followed the lead of the neighboring Catholic congregation and built back in the grand columned classical tradition. This portico received an extensive renovation just a few years back.

Philip Simmons Garden

Working in the ancient hand-forged tradition, Philip Simmons is our best-known ironworker. His gates and trims can be found throughout the city. This garden is a tribute to the man and his work.

Joseph Manigault House
Gifted architect Gabriel Manigault designed this Neoclassical beauty for his brother Joseph in 1803. A gas station was about to take its place when preservationists stepped in at the last moment. The Charleston Museum now operates it as a museum house. The garden has been restored to its earlier splendor. The little gatehouse in the distance once served as a restroom for the adjoining gas station.

Second Presbyterian Church
This church occupies one of the highest spots in the city, and if the proposed steeple had been built, it likely would have been Charleston's highest. It's a deceptive building. Though painted an unobtrusive white, the engaged columns rival those of St. Philip's.

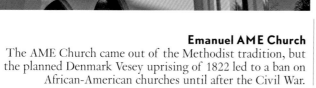

Emanuel AME Church
The AME Church came out of the Methodist tradition, but the planned Denmark Vesey uprising of 1822 led to a ban on African-American churches until after the Civil War.

Grace Episcopal Church
His Huguenout church gets more attention, but E. B. White also designed this Gothic beauty. The original steeple sank; this renovation uses fiberglass finials to reduce the weight.

College of Charleston
Twentieth-century architect Albert Simons added this invitation from Plato's *Dialogues* to Porter's Lodge at the College of Charleston. It translates, "Know thyself."

Bishop's Gate
The Right Reverend Robert Smith, who lived here in the late 18th century, served as South Carolina's first Episcopal bishop and as the first president of the College of Charleston.

Ashley Hall School
The design of this Regency villa is sometimes credited to Savannah architect William Jay. The home's best-known occupant was blockade runner George Trenholm, who's been suggested as the model for Rhett Butler. In 1909 a school was established here. Today, it's a Charleston institution.

Montagu Street Garden
I'm told this handsomely landscaped stretch is a recent addition to the neighborhood. The house was built around 1815 as a home for Dr. North, an intendent, or mayor, of the city and president of the Medical Association.

Columns at Cannon Park (*following spread*)
Built at the end of the 19th century, this convention center went on to house the Charleston Museum. Left vacant, it soon burned, but the columns remain a favorite spot for newlyweds to have their photographs taken.

Francis Silas Rodgers Mansion

Rodgers was a Victorian-era businessman and built this Second Empire mansion to celebrate his successes in phosphate, cotton and coastal shipping. The mansard roof is the defining element of the style. A fire department organizer, Rodgers watched for fires from this cupola and attended every blaze. It's now a popular hotel called the Wentworth Mansion.

Avery Institute

Built in 1867 with this distinctive red brick, Avery was the first free secondary education school for African Americans in the city. Today it operates as a research library and museum.

93

Colonial Lake

In 1768 this site was set aside as a common, that is, land held in common for all people. The lake was a millpond used by sawmills in the area. Some still call it "the pond." The park dates from Victorian times.

Charleston Marina

Charleston has had a longtime tradition of pleasure boating. More than 100 years ago broad work boats called bateaus held hard-fought sailing regattas every year. Here's the modern equivalent. In the distance, an antebellum rice mill, a reminder that Charleston's early wealth came from rice not cotton.

Arthur Ravenel Bridge (*following spread*)

With two soaring diamond-shaped towers, the Ravenel Bridge has given the city a grand new landmark—as well as speeding up traffic and providing pedestrians with miles of breathtaking views.

94

Patriots Point

The massive USS *Yorktown* dominates Patriots Point, a collection of navy ships just over the bridge from downtown Charleston. This tourist and local favorite is among the best-loved and most visited sites in the Lowcountry.

Cypress Gardens

Established in 1931, Cypress Gardens is the perfect place to experience the Lowcountry's romance with wild beauty. Visitors can enjoy cypress swamps bordered by extensive gardens either by boat or path. Plus, there's an archaeology display, "Swamparium" and Butterfly House. And, wedding parties are welcome.

Charles Pinckney House

Revolutionary-era statesman Charles Pinckney hosted General Washington here for breakfast. The plantation is open to the public and gives a good interpretation of black Lowcountry, or Gullah, life. The builder of the 1828 house was a Mr. Matthews whose ferry, through a Gullah transformation, was called Matthis Ferry.

Boone Hall Plantation

Settled in 1681, Boone Hall Plantation has in recent years enjoyed a major revival. The live oak avenue, unique brick slave quarters, formal house garden and mansion provide visitors a full day's entertainment. The plantation plays host to several festivals and an oyster roast, as well as Civil War reenactments. The site has been used in several movies, including *North and South*.

Fort Moultrie at Dawn
The original fort of palmetto logs proved sufficient to repel an English fleet in 1776. "Sir Peter has his breeches shot off," according to a song of the day. The fort was improved and expanded over the years and opened to the public as a national park.

Sullivan's Island Lighthouse
Charleston's revered lighthouse stands sentinel over the coast. The nearby Lifeboat Station dates from 1894 and the unique triangular light from 1962. The lighthouse grounds are open to the public, but trips to the top are restricted.

The Hunley Crew Graves at Magnolia Cemetery

Despite its justifiable reputation as "a coffin," the world's first functioning submarine, the *Hunley*, continued to attract crews. This plot at historic Magnolia Cemetery contains all three crews that perished aboard the *Hunley*. The white stones mark the graves of the final Hunley crew, whose bodies were recovered when the sub was raised from the harbor in 2000. It's easy to spend a day at Magnolia Cemetery, where history and beauty fill every step.

The Citadel

The first home of the Military College of South Carolina was the old Citadel on Marion Square. This campus was a 1918 gift from the city. Dress parades are held on these grounds. A nearby military museum is open to the public.

Middleton Place
The first Henry Middleton received the plantation in 1741 as part of his wife's dowry. Union sailors burned the house except for a flanker building seen here. Today, the attraction offers carriage rides, a crafts-filled barnyard and a restaurant, plus an immense garden of world renown.

Middleton Place Dining Room
The Middleton family has been particularly generous about donating heirlooms of museum quality. Arthur and Mary Izard Middleton acquired this set of eight matched silver candlesticks while touring Europe in the late 18th century. After being scattered among multiple descendents, the candlesticks just recently were reunited to once again light the Middleton Place dining room.

Drayton Hall

Union troops spared this 1738 house on the Ashley River, one of America's finest Georgian-Palladian structures. It is tended by the National Trust for Historic Preservation and open to the public.

Magnolia Gardens

In the late 19th century, garden enthusiasts took steamboats from Charleston to view Reverend Grimke Drayton's free-flowing gardens. It's still easy to spend a day here along the Ashley River.

Tea Plantation
The Charleston Tea Plantation on Wadmalaw Island produces American Classic Tea for Bigelow.
There are more than 100 acres of tea plants, a working tea factory and a gift shop, plus educational trolley tours.
And, lost-in-time Wadmalaw Island is also a treat.

The Angel Oak
The saying goes "a live oak grows for a hundred years, lives for
a hundred years and dies for a hundred years." Here's an amazing exception.
The Angel Oak is over 1,000 years old.

Shrimp Boats
One hundred and twenty years ago, Charleston was America's leading producer of
shrimp. Fishermen still work these waters, but competition from foreign, farm-raised
shrimp and rising fuel prices have drastically reduced the number of shrimp boats.
Those remaining sell the catch as fresh and American-raised.

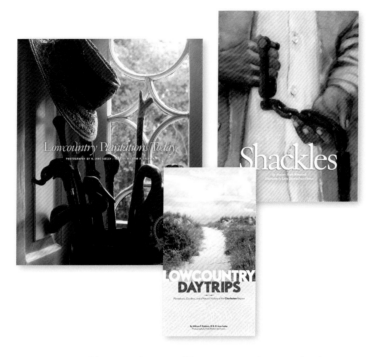

Visit **www.legacypublications.com** for more books
about Charleston and the South Carolina Lowcountry, including . . .

Lowcountry Plantations Today
Charleston
The Charleston Interior
Lowcountry Day Trips
Charleston Entertains
Lowcountry: The Natural Landscape
Plantations of the Lowcountry

Hermy the Hermit Crab and the Sea Turtle Rescue
Mr. Gator Hits the Beach
Shackles
Rosebud Roams Charleston